Let Freedom Ring

Dorothea Dix

Social Reformer

by Barbara Witteman

Consultant:
Marjorie L. O'Rorke
Historian
Dorothea Dix Hospital, Raleigh, North Carolina

Bridgestone Books
an imprint of Capstone Press
Mankato, Minnesota

Bridgestone Books are published by Capstone Press
151 Good Counsel Drive, PO Box 669, Mankato, Minnesota 56002
http://www.capstone-press.com

Library of Congress Cataloging-in-Publication Data
Witteman, Barbara.
    Dorothea Dix: Social reformer / by Barbara Witteman.
    p. cm.—(Let freedom ring)
    Summary: A biography of the nineteenth-century reformer who devoted much of her life to improving the treatment of the mentally ill in the United States.
    ISBN 0-7368-1552-X (hardcover)
    1. Dix, Dorothea Lynde, 1802–1887—Juvenile literature. 2. Women social reformers—United States—Juvenile literature. 3. Mentally ill—Care—United States—History—Juvenile literature. [1. Dix, Dorothea Lynde, 1802–1887. 2. Reformers. 3. Women—Biography. 4. Mentally ill—Care—History.] I. Title. II. Series.
HV28.D6 W57 2003
361.92—dc21
                                                                2002012011

Editorial Credits
Rebecca Glaser, editor; Kia Adams, series designer; Juliette Peters, book designer;
    Kelly Garvin, photo researcher; Karen Risch, product planning editor

Photo Credits
Corbis, cover (main); Francis G. Mayer, 15; Richard T. Nowitz, 19; Hulton-Deutsch
    Collection, 30; Medford Historical Society Collection, 34
Courtesy of Fort Monroe Casemate Museum, 37
Courtesy of the National Library of Medicine, 23
Courtesy of the University of Liverpool Library, 20
Houghton Library, Harvard University, 9, 11, 39, 41, 42
Hulton Archive by Getty Images, 13, 33
Illinois State Historical Library, 24
J.N. Stearns and Co./Capstone Press Archives, 19
National Portrait Gallery/Smithsonian Institution, 5
North Carolina Office of Archives and History, 41
North Wind Picture Archives, 7, 16
Trenton Psychiatric Hospital, cover (inset), 26
U.S. Postal Service, 43

1   2   3   4   5   6   0 8   0 7   0 6   0 5   0 4   0 3

Table of Contents

Chapter One

A Mission

In March 1841, Dorothea Dix finished teaching a Sunday school class in a Massachusetts prison. She toured the East Cambridge Jail after her class and was disgusted by the conditions she saw.

Dorothea noticed that mentally ill people who had not committed any crime were in jail. She asked the guard why the cells for the mentally ill were not heated. He replied that mentally ill people could not feel the heat. Dorothea was outraged, and she went to court to fight for better conditions in the jail. She eventually convinced a judge to order heat in the cells.

The East Cambridge Jail tour sparked a sense of mission in Dorothea.

Dorothea Dix wrote reports called memorials to the governments in many states, asking them to fund hospitals for the mentally ill.

She traveled to other jails in Massachusetts and wrote a report of her findings to the Massachusetts government. This memorial convinced the lawmakers to expand a hospital for the mentally ill.

Dorothea continued to campaign for hospitals where the mentally ill could receive better care. She lobbied state governments to provide funding for state hospitals. People across the country began to recognize her name as a crusader for the mentally ill and as a social reformer. She traveled to almost every state in the United States and several countries in Europe. She never returned to her birthplace of Hampden, Maine.

Treatment of the Mentally Ill

In the early 1800s, people with mental illnesses were called insane or lunatic. Many people who were labeled as insane in Dorothea's time would be considered normal today. Few hospitals existed to help the mentally ill. Many mentally ill people were put in jail, and people forgot about them. People thought that mental illness was a disgrace. Family members who suffered from it were hidden. Many people believed that mental illness was a punishment for sins. Some thought the mentally ill had diseased intestines or brain cells. Because no one knew how to effectively treat mental illness, these people often did not receive medical care.

In 1840, there were 17,434 people labeled as mentally ill in the United States. Some states provided asylums staffed by doctors or other places for the mentally ill to live. Some places had only guards. Any person looking for a job could get one in an asylum. The workers were often afraid of the inmates, so the guards used straitjackets, balls and chains, iron collars, and even cages to restrain the patients.

Chapter Two

Girlhood

Dorothy Lynde Dix was born in Hampden, Maine, on April 4, 1802. Her parents were Joseph and Mary Dix. Her parents called her Dolly when she was young. Dorothy was named after her grandmother, who was also called Dolly. As Dorothy grew up, she wanted to become more independent. When she turned 22, she renamed herself Dorothea. Dorothea was the oldest child in her family. She had two younger brothers. Charles Wesley was born in 1812, and Joseph was born in 1815.

Dorothea's Parents

Dorothea's mother was a sickly person who seemed unhappy and unloving. Dorothea learned to take care of herself because she was left alone much of the time. She often went on long walks in the fields near her home. Her parents did not usually notice

At age 22, Dorothea changed her name from Dorothy to Dorothea. She did not like having the same name as her grandmother.

In Her Own Words

After Dorothea grew up, she seldom spoke of the childhood she called a "time of loneliness and despair." She did not feel loved by her parents. She later wrote, "I never had a childhood," because she did not want to remember that time of her life.

that she was gone. Dorothea's mother became sick after Joseph's birth and could not take care of the family. Dorothea cared for her mother and two younger brothers.

Dorothea's father, Joseph, was not successful. He did not appear to care much about his family. Joseph's father, a wealthy man from Boston, gave Joseph and Mary land in Maine. But Joseph failed at farming and did not manage the land carefully. The Dix family moved many times during Dorothea's childhood.

Joseph became a bookseller. He printed some of the booklets, or tracts, that he sold. Joseph sometimes traded tracts for food. These books were not bound with hard covers. Dorothea and her mother folded and sewed the bindings of the printed tracts. Dorothea hated this job.

A New Life

When Dorothea was 12, her family visited Worcester, Massachusetts. While there, Dorothea ran away to her grandmother's house in Boston. Boston was located 40 miles (64 kilometers) from Worcester. Dorothea lived with her grandmother, Madame Dix, for about two years. They did not always get along. Madame Dix wanted to teach Dorothea good

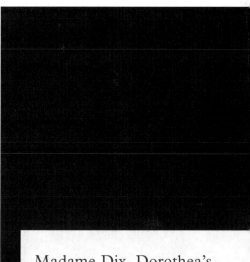

Madame Dix, Dorothea's grandmother, was often strict with Dorothea.

manners and proper rules for etiquette. Dorothea did not like her grandmother's strict rules. In 1816, Madame Dix arranged for Dorothea to move to Worcester.

Living in Worcester

Dorothea lived in Worcester for about four years in the home of her grandmother's sister, Sarah Lynde Fiske. Here, Dorothea finally met people her own age. She enjoyed visiting with her cousins. She became friends with her older cousin, Edward Bangs, who was a lawyer.

Many young girls started teaching to show that they were grown up. They held dame schools in their homes or other buildings. In 1816, Dorothea started a school in Worcester when she was 14 years old. She wore long skirts and pinned her hair up to look older. Dorothea enjoyed teaching, but she also wanted more education for herself. After about four years in Worcester, she moved to Boston to live once again with her grandmother.

Dame Schools

Dame schools were common in Boston from 1820 to 1835. Women held these private schools in their homes to teach reading and spelling. Parents paid for their children to attend dame schools. Many students entered dame schools at age 4. Once they learned to read and spell, students could enter public school at age 7.

Chapter Three

Teaching Days

When Dorothea returned to Boston in 1819, she wanted to teach again. Madame Dix thought that Dorothea was not strong enough to teach. Dorothea finally convinced her grandmother to let her open a school in a room over the stable. Students could attend this school for free. At the same time, she held a separate school for children of wealthy families, also on her grandmother's property. Dorothea earned money from the tuition that parents paid.

Dorothea loved teaching and working with the children. She studied hard and went to lectures to become an even better teacher.

As a teacher, Dorothea was strict. She wanted her students to do their best and behave perfectly. Dorothea's students wrote about their personal weaknesses in journals. Dorothea read their journals, wrote back and gave advice to her students.

Dorothea held schools like this one in a room over her grandmother's stable.

A New Job and Church

In 1824, Dorothea began teaching needlework at another private school. She had 70 students. Most of them were between 7 and 12 years old. She was still teaching her school at Madame Dix's house. She worked many hours each day at both schools.

Dorothea began attending a Unitarian church in Boston. She enjoyed listening to the sermons of the pastor, Dr. William Ellery Channing. She and Dr. Channing became lifelong friends.

Dr. William Ellery Channing was a friend of Dorothea. They met at the Unitarian church where he was pastor.

Illness and Life Changes

Dorothea kept herself busy. She read the Bible before breakfast. After teaching all day, Dorothea studied at night to become a better teacher. She wrote in her students' journals until after midnight.

After three years of constant work, her body was run down. Her doctor told her she had rheumatism of the lungs, which later became known as tuberculosis. This serious illness affected Dorothea's lungs and made breathing difficult. She had to stop teaching to recover from her illness. Dorothea wrote books and poetry during this time.

Dorothea and her grandmother did not get along well. Madame Dix was strict and hard to please. Dorothea's brother Charles also moved to live with Madame Dix. Dorothea and her grandmother often disagreed about how to raise him. Because of their strained relationship, Dorothea did not want to have the same name as her grandmother. She said that when she heard the name Dolly, it sounded foreign. She changed her name to Dorothea.

In 1827, Dr. Channing hired Dorothea to tutor his two children. She spent the summer with the

Conch Shell Mailbox

Dorothea taught her students to write letters and to think about their lives. She encouraged these acts by using a conch shell from St. Croix as a mailbox. Her students wrote letters to her and put them in the shell. She wrote back to her students with suggestions for self-improvement. One letter from a student read: "You know, dear Miss Dix, that I told you just now that I could not do my composition, and ... I just read ... 'An iron will can accomplish everything.' Dear Miss Dix, I will have this 'iron will' and I will do and be all you expect from your child."

Channing family at Portsmouth, Rhode Island. In 1830, Dorothea traveled to St. Croix in the Virgin Islands with the Channing family.

Teaching Again

Dorothea returned to Boston in 1831. She opened a combined day and boarding school for girls in Madame Dix's house. Some local students came to school only for the day. Students from farther away could live in rooms at the school. Dorothea taught character education, morals, and religion in addition to reading, writing, mathematics, and science. In 1835, Dorothea started a charity school in a building on her grandmother's property.

Busy with her two schools, Dorothea was again wearing down. She often suffered from headaches. She did not take good care of herself. In 1836, Dorothea suffered a complete physical and nervous collapse. Her schools had to close. Dorothea was not strong enough to work so hard without rest. Her doctor told her to travel to Europe to rest. The rough sea voyage made her more ill.

Students in Dorothea's classes may have used books and magazines similar to these.

Living in Europe

When Dorothea arrived in Liverpool, England, she went straight to a hotel bed. An English friend of Dr. Channing, William Rathbone, heard that Dorothea was ill. Rathbone moved Dorothea into his country home called Greenbank. Dorothea became friends with several members of the family.

While Dorothea was still in England, Madame Dix died on April 29, 1837. Dorothea felt alone. Her father had died in 1821, and her mother had

During her trip to Europe, Dorothea stayed with the Rathbones at their home called Greenbank, in England.

died in 1834. Her brother Charles was at sea. She did not keep in touch with her youngest brother, Joseph.

In 1837, Dorothea returned to Boston. Her health would not allow her to spend so much time teaching. Her grandmother had left her some money, so Dorothea did not have to work.

New Purpose in Life

Dorothea began to search for a new purpose in her life. In March 1841, she heard that a Sunday school teacher was needed for 20 female prisoners in Boston's East Cambridge Jail. She volunteered for the job. After holding her first Sunday school class, Dorothea walked through the jail.

Dorothea saw the mentally ill people who were imprisoned. The criminals in jail had better living conditions than the mentally ill did.

Dorothea went to court to make the jail improve conditions for the mentally ill prisoners. The jailer agreed to put in a stove for heat. Dorothea had found a new purpose in life. She would help the mentally ill.

Chapter Four

Lobbyist for the Mentally Ill

Dorothea decided to visit other jails near Cambridge. Some conditions were even worse than at the East Cambridge Jail. She set a goal to visit every jail in Massachusetts.

Campaigning in Massachusetts

Dorothea kept written records of what she saw. She wrote that the mentally ill were "confined in cages, closets, cellars, stalls, pens! Chained, naked, beaten with rods..." Dorothea saw people who were neglected and filthy. Mentally ill people often had no sinks, bathtubs, or toilets. Their clothing was thin. They received no medical help.

Within 18 months, Dorothea had visited every prison, workhouse, and almshouse in Massachusetts. Poor people, including the mentally ill, lived in almshouses. Workhouses were prisons where the inmates had to work.

In Dorothea's time, mentally ill people were sometimes kept in cages.

Dorothea lobbied, or tried to convince, lawmakers to change conditions at these places. Her final report was called a memorial. The lawmakers of the time were men and were unlikely to listen to women. Dorothea found a man to present her memorial.

Samuel Gridley Howe presented Dorothea's *Memorial to the Massachusetts Legislature* in January 1843. It was printed in pamphlet form so people could read it. Newspapers printed parts of it. Many people thought that Dorothea had made up the stories.

Dorothea helped campaign for this asylum built in Jacksonville, Illinois. When it was built, she picked out the pictures hanging in the hallways.

In Her Words

Dorothea kept careful records of what she saw in the places she visited. One of her entries was from Groton, Massachusetts, 40 miles (64 kilometers) northwest of Boston. She visited the poorhouse there and described one man's condition in her *Memorial to the Massachusetts Legislature.*

"...There is no window, save an opening half the size of the sash, and closed by a board shutter; in one corner is some brickwork surrounding an iron stove, which in cold weather serves for warming the room. The occupant of this [room] is a young man, who has been declared incurably mentally ill. He can move a measured distance in his prison; that is, so far as a strong, heavy chain [descending] from an iron collar which [surrounds] his neck permits..."

Dorothea did not give up. She kept trying to convince people. After a committee report, the legislature passed a bill to expand the Worcester State Lunatic Asylum to hold 150 more people.

Work in Other States

After her success in Massachusetts, Dorothea traveled to other states. She wrote memorials in several states. She also spoke personally to many lawmakers and convinced them to support state hospitals for the mentally ill. Dorothea did not take any pay for her work. She stayed with friends. Transportation companies gave her free passage.

People heard about Dorothea's work and often knew who she was even before she introduced herself. Some people wrote to her and asked for

Dorothea believed that the location of the New Jersey State Lunatic Asylum, on a hill overlooking scenic land near Trenton, would be peaceful for patients.

help in their states. She was one of the most influential women in the politics of her time.

New Hospitals

Dorothea was happy when the New Jersey State Lunatic Asylum was built. She was there when it opened on May 15, 1848. Dorothea spoke like a mother about the hospital, calling it her "first-born child." She had been involved with the hospital from the beginning. It was the first hospital for the mentally ill in New Jersey.

Dorothea also traveled to North Carolina in 1848. She visited jails, almshouses, and private homes where the mentally ill lived. She wrote a memorial to the state government, asking for a new state hospital. At first, the government said no because of the cost.

While living in Raleigh, North Carolina, Dorothea cared for an important politician's wife, Louisa Dobbins. On her deathbed, Dobbins asked her husband to support Dorothea's bill. Because of his support, the bill passed, and the first state hospital in North Carolina was created. Hospital officials wanted to name the hospital after Dorothea, but she refused. More than 100 years later, the hospital was renamed Dorothea Dix Hospital.

Lobbying the U.S. Congress

Dorothea had observed the conditions of the mentally ill in many states. She thought that the federal government should become involved. The government owned much land that could be sold. Dorothea thought that money from the sale of this land could be used to support state mental hospitals.

Dorothea wrote a memorial to Congress in 1848, stating facts about the conditions for the mentally ill in the nation. She argued that the federal government should provide money to care for the mentally ill. State hospitals could not depend only on local funding. She asked two congressmen to present her memorial to Congress. After they presented it, a committee was formed to study the issue.

A bill was written based on Dorothea's memorial. Many people were trying to get funds from public land at that time. Congress could not agree on how to use the land. Congress postponed Dorothea's bill several times. Dorothea met with congressmen and tried to convince them to vote for her bill. In 1854, the bill was finally defeated.

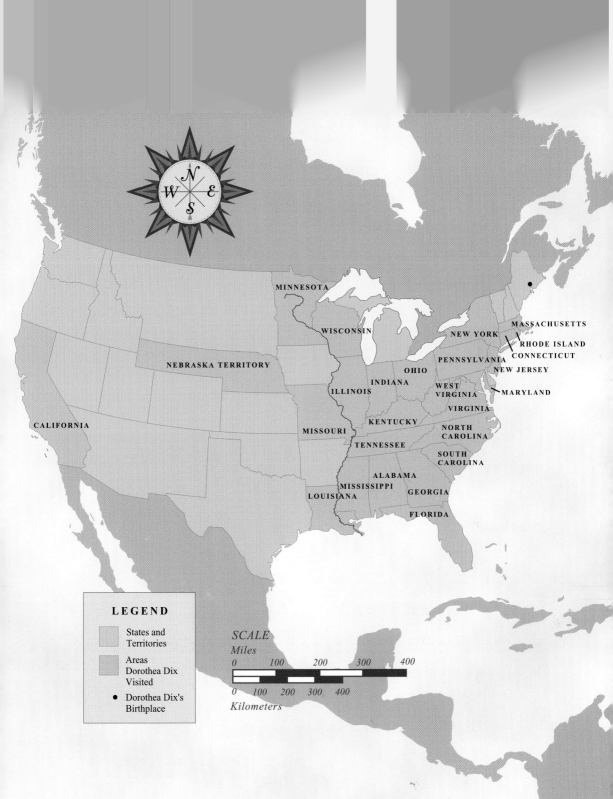

MINNESOTA

WISCONSIN

NEBRASKA TERRITORY

CALIFORNIA

NEW YORK

MASSACHUSETTS

RHODE ISLAND
CONNECTICUT

PENNSYLVANIA

NEW JERSEY

OHIO

MARYLAND

INDIANA

WEST
VIRGINIA

ILLINOIS

VIRGINIA

MISSOURI

KENTUCKY

NORTH
CAROLINA

TENNESSEE

SOUTH
CAROLINA

ALABAMA

MISSISSIPPI

GEORGIA

LOUISIANA

FLORIDA

LEGEND

States and
Territories

Areas
Dorothea Dix
Visited

● Dorothea Dix's
Birthplace

SCALE
Miles

0   100   200   300   400

0   100   200   300   400
Kilometers

29

Work in Europe

Dorothea traveled to Europe again in 1854. After visiting friends in England, she went to Scotland and traveled to the places where the mentally ill stayed. She talked to British officials in London and convinced them to investigate the asylums in Scotland, which Great Britain controlled at the time. She argued that doctors should lead asylums, instead of people with no medical knowledge.

Continuing her work in Europe, Dorothea visited Italy, France, Turkey, and Russia. She also

Pope Pius IX received a visit from Dorothea in the 1850s. He listened to her report about the conditions of asylums in Rome.

went to Sweden, Norway, Denmark, Holland, and parts of Germany and Belgium. In Rome, she met with Pope Pius IX. She told him that the asylum in Rome was "a scandal and a disgrace." After visiting the place himself, the Pope ordered that a new hospital be built. In the fall of 1856, Dorothea returned to the United States.

Back Home

At home, Dorothea continued her work. She met with state politicians. She talked many of them into approving public funds to buy land for hospitals for the mentally ill and to build hospitals. Dorothea asked private citizens for money and materials. She received books, toys, and clothing for the hospitals.

The 1850s were a time of growing tension in the United States. States in the South were in favor of states' rights. They wanted to decide whether to have slaves in their states. Many people in the North believed slavery was wrong. These abolitionists thought the national government should outlaw slavery. The issues of slavery and states' rights led to the Civil War (1861–1865). Dorothea did not take sides on the issue.

Chapter Five

Civil War Nursing

President Abraham Lincoln asked for 75,000 volunteers to support the northern states in the Civil War. Although Dorothea was nearly 60 years old, she traveled to the White House to volunteer. Lincoln accepted her offer. On June 10, 1861, she was named the Superintendent of Women Nurses for the U.S. Army.

Dorothea's War Reputation

Dorothea set to work. She asked the women of the North to make bandages and hospital clothing. She also asked women to sign up to be nurses.

Dorothea had learned a great deal from inspecting hospitals, but she had not learned how to nurse. She knew it would be hard work. Dorothea listed her rules for women who wished to be nurses. "No woman under 30 need apply to serve in the government hospitals. All nurses are required to be

Civil War nurses cared for many patients in hospitals like this one in Washington, D.C.

very plain-looking women. Their dresses must be brown or black, with no bows, no curls, no jewelry, and no hoop-skirts." Dorothea set her rules to protect the women nurses. She worried that male doctors and soldiers would be distracted by pretty nurses.

Many people called Dorothea a spinster, a negative term given to unmarried women. Other people laughed at Dorothea's strict rules. People called her "Dragon Dix." In reality, Dorothea did not strictly enforce her rules. Nurses dressed in other colors than black or brown. Pretty women were nurses. Some nurses were younger than 30 years old.

Dorothea supervised nurses in this building, which was used as a hospital during the Civil War.

Hard Work

Dorothea worked every day during the war. During August 1861, when she was sick, she gave orders from her bed. Dorothea wanted them followed without question. She stated, "I think even lying on my bed I can still do something."

Dorothea acted like a mother to her nurses. She opened the home she rented in Washington, D.C., to the nurses so they could rest when they were off duty. If they were sick, Dorothea made sure they got special care.

Dorothea pushed to make things better for patients in the hospitals. She offered comments to everyone on how they could improve. Some people were offended. She was also quick to anger when hospital conditions were not good. Dorothea said what she thought and did not care if she upset others. Some doctors tried to have her fired. Others respected what Dorothea tried to do.

Conflict also happened in other government positions. The secretary of war did not like the surgeon general, who was in charge of the army nurses and doctors. The secretary of war, Edwin

Stanton, chose a new surgeon general named Joseph Barnes. Barnes did not want Dorothea to have authority over the nurses. In October 1863, Dorothea was no longer allowed to assign nurses unless she got approval from a surgeon. The new surgeon general now chose most nurses and assigned them to certain posts. Dorothea pretended that she had not lost this authority. She continued to help during the Civil War and did not resign until after the war was over.

War's End

When the war ended, Dorothea stayed in Washington, D.C., for four months. She worked in hospitals. She helped soldiers contact their families.

In August 1865, Dorothea resigned as Superintendent of Women Nurses. Secretary of war Edwin Stanton asked her how she would like to be thanked. Dorothea asked for a flag.

Dorothea did not want to be remembered for her Civil War work. She wrote, "This is not the work I would have my life judged by!" She destroyed many of her personal papers relating to this time.

Later, when she wrote her will, she asked that her wartime letters and papers not be published.

After the Civil War, Dorothea helped with a monument project at Fortress Monroe in Virginia. The monument honored soldiers from the northern states who died during the Civil War. Dorothea raised $8,000 to pay for the monument. She also chose the granite herself and designed a fence made of rifles around the stone monument.

Dorothea helped raise money for this Civil War monument in Hampton National Cemetery, in Hampton, Virginia.

Chapter Six

Later Years

Dorothea returned to her mission to help the mentally ill after the Civil War. She soon discovered that the number of patients had increased while the size of the state hospitals had not. She wrote a memorial to the Connecticut legislature to help establish a state hospital there. She campaigned in New York. Dorothea traveled to the West Coast with friends and visited jails and state hospitals along the way.

In October 1881, Dorothea returned to the Trenton, New Jersey, hospital. She had a fever and pain in her lung and collapsed when she arrived. She was too ill to travel anymore. The hospital's staff invited her to spend the rest of her life with them. While living at the hospital, Dorothea slowly lost her hearing and much of her sight.

Even in later life, Dorothea did not give up her mission.
She continued writing memorials as long as she could.

Great Moment: Hall of Fame

Dorothea was named to the American Nurses Association Hall of Fame in 1976. She was honored for her work in helping the mentally ill. To win this award, nurses must show leadership. They must also have made lasting changes to the nursing profession.

Dorothea died at age 85 on July 18, 1887. Dr. Charles Nichols, whom Dorothea worked with to improve the state hospital in New York, spoke at her funeral. He called her "the most powerful and distinguished woman America has yet produced." She is buried in the Mount Auburn Cemetery in Boston. The flags of the United States and of the Corps of Army Nurses fly over her grave. The marker simply reads "Dorothea L. Dix."

Dorothea is remembered for her work lobbying governments to provide state hospitals for the mentally ill. When she started her work in 1841, there were 13 asylums. In 1880, there were 123 asylums. Dorothea helped start 32 of them. She did her best to help in the ways she knew how.

Dorothea's writings helped convince lawmakers to increase the number of hospitals for the mentally ill.

TIMELINE

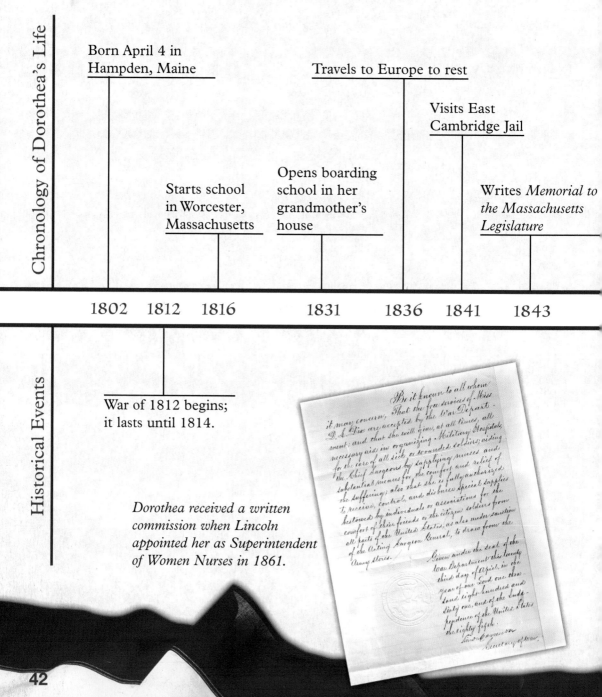

Chronology of Dorothea's Life

Born April 4 in Hampden, Maine

Travels to Europe to rest

Visits East Cambridge Jail

Starts school in Worcester, Massachusetts

Opens boarding school in her grandmother's house

Writes *Memorial to the Massachusetts Legislature*

| 1802 | 1812 | 1816 | 1831 | 1836 | 1841 | 1843 |

Historical Events

War of 1812 begins; it lasts until 1814.

Dorothea received a written commission when Lincoln appointed her as Superintendent of Women Nurses in 1861.

Dorothea Dix
USA 1c

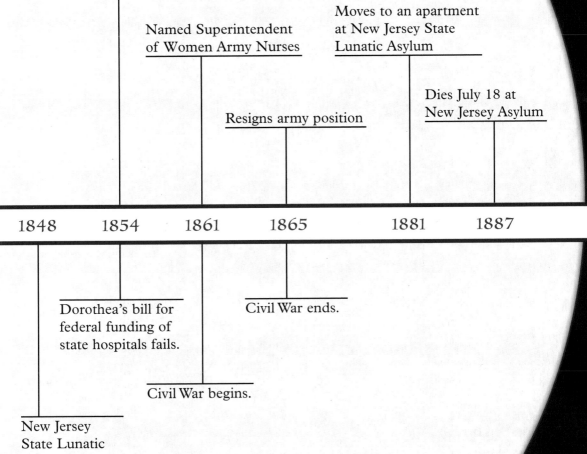

Visits Europe again and
tours hospitals and jails

Named Superintendent
of Women Army Nurses

Moves to an apartment
at New Jersey State
Lunatic Asylum

Resigns army position

Dies July 18 at
New Jersey Asylum

| 1848 | 1854 | 1861 | 1865 | 1881 | 1887 |

Dorothea's bill for
federal funding of
state hospitals fails.

Civil War ends.

Civil War begins.

New Jersey
State Lunatic
Asylum opens.

Glossary

almshouse (ALMZ-houss)—a privately owned place where poor people lived in the 1700s and 1800s

asylum (uh-SYE-luhm)—a hospital for people who are mentally ill and cannot live alone

dame school (DAYM SKOOL)—a school in early American times run by a woman from her home

etiquette (ET-uh-ket)—rules of polite behavior and manners, such as the proper way to eat in public or the proper way to introduce yourself to someone

lobby (LOB-ee)—to try to persuade government officials to act or vote in a certain way

memorial (muh-MOR-ee-uhl)—a term used in Dorothea's time to describe a report requesting changes

pamphlet (PAM-flit)—a small printed booklet that contains information on one topic

social reformer (SOH-shuhl re-FORM-ur)—someone who works to improve something in society

tuberculosis (tu-bur-kyuh-LOH-siss)—a serious and contagious lung disease caused by bacteria; tuberculosis makes breathing difficult.

workhouse (WORK-houss)—a prison where inmates have to work

For Further Reading

Herstek, Amy Paulson. *Dorothea Dix: Crusader for the Mentally Ill.* Historical American Biographies. Berkeley Heights, N.J.: Enslow Publishers, 2001.

Savage, Douglas. *Civil War Medicine.* Untold History of the Civil War. Philadelphia: Chelsea House Publishers, 2000.

Shura, Mary Francis. *Gentle Annie: The True Story of a Civil War Nurse.* New York: Apple, 1997.

Wilbur, C. Keith. *Civil War Medicine, 1861–1865.* Illustrated Living History Series. Philadelphia: Chelsea House Publishers, 1999.

Places of Interest

American Nurses Association Hall of Fame
600 Maryland Avenue SW
Suite 100 West
Washington, DC 20024-2571

This museum honors all nurses who have been named to the nursing Hall of Fame.

Dorothea Dix Library and Museum
Harrisburg State Hospital
Cameron and McClay Streets
Harrisburg, PA 17105-1300

This museum has artifacts and exhibits showing the history of mental health treatment in Pennsylvania. Dorothea helped to raise funds for the reading room.

Dorothea Dix Hospital
820 South Boylan Avenue
Raleigh, NC 27603-2176

An exhibit in the lobby tells about the founding of this hospital, including Dorothea's role.

Mount Auburn Cemetery
580 Mount Auburn Street
Cambridge, MA 02138-5529

The graves of many notable people, including Dorothea, can be found at this cemetery.

Internet Sites

Do you want to learn more about Dorothea Dix?
Visit the FACT HOUND at *http://www.facthound.com*.

FACT HOUND can track down many sites to help you.
All the FACT HOUND sites are hand-selected
by Capstone Press editors. FACT HOUND will fetch the
best, most accurate information to answer your questions.

IT IS EASY! IT IS FUN!
1) Go to *http://www.facthound.com*
2) Type in: 073681552X
3) Click on "FETCH IT" and
   FACT HOUND will put you on
   the trail of several helpful links.

You can also search by subject or book title. So, relax
and let our pal FACT HOUND do the research for you!

Index